The Edge of
Known Things

The Edge of
Known Things

Kelly Madigan

For Jennifer & Greg, on their anniversary.

—Kelly Madigan

STEPHEN F. AUSTIN STATE UNIVERSITY PRESS

NACOGDOCHES ◆ TEXAS

Stephen F. Austin State University Press
P.O. Box 13007, SFA Station
Nacogdoches, TX   75962-3007
sfasu.edu/sfapress
sfapress@sfasu.edu

Book Design: Laura Davis
Cover Art: "The Illuminated One" © Aleta Braun, 2004
Author photo: Tara Polly

Manufactured in the United States of America

LIBRARY OF CONGRESS IN PUBLICATION DATA
Madigan, Kelly
The Edge of Known Things / Kelly Madigan

p. cm.
ISBN: 978-1-62288-008-9

1. Poetry. 2. American Poetry 3. Kelly Madigan

Distributed by Texas A&M Consortium
www.tamupress.com

CONTENTS

Dedicated to my mother, Marion Madigan, who showed the way by making art.

Things throw light on things.
— Theodore Roethke

Mnemosyne's Mausoleum

Tobacco smell and the taste of buttered parsnips
are stored in far flung coffins in the brain,
a catacomb of sensory descriptions
that the tiniest encounter disinters.
They all lie down together, and if left unstirred
by mice, or brush of garment whooshing by,
the sense of steamy water on bare skin
can mix with coyotes waking up the night.
The crossover of memory, forming new
experiences that never really were
can make a bookstore lush with trumpet vine,
or layer frozen windows in the car
with licorice, or mango, on the tongue.
The hybrid of this intermingled storage
can trick the ear that thinks it hears a train,
make it think, instead, of the underwater language
of blue whales, or babies crying in their beds.
We've pressed our rich collection
into such slim space. If the shine of coreopsis
is now blocked by blankets on the line,
or drive-in movie screens, it means
the world we travel backwards through
has a deeper depth of field than when we came.

OFFERING

Always the same story—
the bulldozers at the meadow's edge,
the high whine of motorized saws
at the base of nests.

Always my heart beating
in the sole of my foot,
the tire on the economy van
from the city's poorest church
about to blow on the blacktop
with fourteen children inside.

The banks of the river
are hung with trash
and even now a little ways
upstream a boy kicks
the Styrofoam bait container
into the brown water.

Spring comes too early
or not at all, the bees have fled
and someone quotes Einstein,
and someone else comes along
to say he never really said that,
but it rings in your ears
anyway, the bee-dead earth.

We steal each other's jewelry
and one gets drunk and says
what he has held back for years
while another pours ammonia
into the watershed
and the fish are gaping at the edges.

Throw open the pasture gates
and let the horses have their heads,
allow them to cross the river
in the dark. Light fire to the altars
and throw on sage and cedar
and the long list of grievances.

No one can autopsy the bees
since they never return to the hive.
They dispute the Einstein quote,
say it is overblown. The bees
are rich and plentiful,
they are high on the hog,
they are in greener fields.

In the black cave
of the forest, the growl
and heave of heavy equipment.
I can see the path
the deer make as they flee.

My palms are turned up
as I place the baby
at the feet of God, as I place
the whole and sleeping baby
in the cradle at the feet
of the everlasting God.

ANOTHER WORD FOR LEAVING

There is smoke rising.
There is a circle made from the bark of trees.
There is deer scat
scattered among the new blades
of switch grass. There is a small wedding
under a magnolia tree, there is a scent
memory of moss hanging from the live oaks.
There is a bee too early for the season.
Every last surface fretted with pollen,
I walk out anyway. At the muddy bank
I rip the hem away from my skirt
and feed it into the water. Don't waver
or turn back. We must do these things
while we still can, while
our mothers are alive, while the road
is still dark. The route is marked by pages
torn from textbooks, marked by lace,
marked by abandoned cars.
In the back seat of the Ford Galaxie
a young boy sleeps in a nest of blue rags.
Even if you lifted him
you could not save him. Like everyone
he has to save himself.

There is no rescue. Remember
the space under the dock,
the smell of wood and algae,
the way we surfaced exactly
between above and beneath,
how I kissed you and said I didn't,
the shadows of big fish moving beneath us.
Later the engine wouldn't start
and you used a long pole
to push us across the lake
in the wooden boat. Remember my silver
bracelet that slipped away,

how I dove under over and over
to find it. The man on the dock said
a meteor had fallen into the lake
when he was young, a sizzling sound
that boiled up for hours after. I walk
the edges of craters now for a living,
I sit at the spine of the continent.
I plan to strap on scuba gear,
breathe artificial air.
You are invited to meet me
in my father's cave. Extinguish all light.
There will be stairs at first,
and a railing you can hold, and afterward
you can follow the sound
of water, the sound of breathing,
the sound of a million bats
awakening, their thin wings
another word for leaving,
another way to say *ground cloth*,
a bandage, a tarp to throw
over the past, an uncapped well.
Meet me there and bring a musical
instrument. Bring bread.
Meet me there on the first day of April.
Meet me and I will tell you
what you have been asking me for years.

Land Contract

A puzzle of a white turtle shell
on the bank of a triangle of water
a man could not coerce
his daughters into keeping.

Trust or no trust.

I am new here, puzzling out
my own deadlocks. Red winged
saints file the sky
with their edged call.

His wife's goods are rotting
in the root cellar.
I am a girl
halfway through, fracturing
under the weight of my life.

My white kayak
on the blackened water
a shell between
me and the remainder.

INVESTIGATION

You circle in the road
ahead of me.

The viaduct bows over you
and beneath you wheels spin.

I barely have a handle on this.
Under the bridge, you point out

the spot for finding bodies.
I concentrate on shifting.

A woman who looks like a man
clears rubbage from the boulevard.

We are past her before
I can tell you her story,

her son who loved horses
until fast cars turned his head.

She's been mad at me
since 1997, but her head was down.

You ride like an investigator
and I have nothing to pedal or give away.

I would turn back and take up her hands,
tell her she raised champions,

but we are past all that and the road
turns to marshland before us.

You say you'll go first and yell
back instructions about where it is soft.

There is a balled-up shirt in the mud.
But to stop now risks everything.

THE ONSET OF MEMORY

A woman says she remembers her own birth,
and this is the primary reason
she cannot work to feed herself
but must rest in the afternoons
with a cool cloth over her forehead.

She talks about her birth at odd times—
the sensation of air replacing water
like coming up out of the sea
from skin diving, water streaming
over the crown of her head.

She raises the story, an umbrella
that fails to shield her. Always the intrusion
of recollection, the assault of a multitude
of colors after the dim interior,
the screech and clank of the world.
Ever since, she has found the human voice
too precise. Swimming underwater
provides some relief, and certain medications
kept in large supply at her bedside.

This is the way the world has damaged her,
the curse of memory starting its engine
prematurely. Always she seeks forgetfulness:
lying down in the snowdrift; throwing coins
into the coated throats of slot machines;
rearranging her red dishes
in the safety of the cupboards. Still, her bones
recall the crush, the headaches come,
and she retreats to the canopied bed,
curtains pulled close like a membrane,
the pendulum clock a second heartbeat
overriding her own.

QUITTING

The boss's office door is closed. No one goes
in or out of the boss's office. Walk the hallway
all the way to its end to find the boss's office.
Nettles are tangled with poppies just outside
the boss's office. The boss's office chair
raises like a forklift before he says, "Come in."

She slides her note under the boss's office door.
It is on rust colored paper, with wet black ink.
It says *the sky is falling*. It says *the fawn has curled
up on the forest floor*. It says *how can I come back
when my arms are already so full?* The note
has saddle burrs tucked under the edges.
It says *I do not do this in haste*.

The boss's office is a steamy place. Carnivorous
plants thrive in the boss's office. Knife-throwers
practice in the boss's office at night. His back goes out
when he leans over to pick up her note. The boss ices
his lumbar spine in his office. The clock in the boss's
office is fast. He likes to think he's late when he's not.

BEFORE SHE DECIDES

They are in a dark plum thicket
and she is too far above the ground,
can feel the lift and fall of walking
but is not walking. Beneath her
are the shoulders of a boy
who is willing to carry her for years

but he is unsteady as a shirt
unbuttoned in the wind, and she
is like a feather on the surface
of a river with round stones
in its bed. She already knows
he will fall, and because she is above
him she will fall further.

But that doesn't matter yet,
the night held up around her
like great bolts of cloth for her choosing.

Negative Capability

He was the boy who outlined the girl's house
with gasoline, after she said *no more.*

In him, every sadness grew a shell
until it was a cold stone

he could let drop from an overpass
onto oncoming traffic beneath him.

Instead of Telling

This is where I don't tell the secrets.
Instead I layer words like *impetigo*
and *multitudinous* to form a field of dirt
where boys who are supposed to be at practice
have found a dead possum and a stick.
Or divide *shelterbelt* by *underhand*
to recreate a basement bathroom
with no door, the light controlled
by pull chains that can't be reached.
This is where I take *First Holy Communion*
and cross it with *bedwetter* to reflect
the girl who threw herself to the ground
writhing rather than go to gym. Where
usual burdens intersect with *hammered*
dulcimer to say never again, or save me.
Where *wooden ladder* thrown against
high fence blows wide the old songbook.
We know the lyrics, but have been taught
to whistle instead of sing, the mouth
round with sound, the tiny opening
unsuited for consonants.

COYOTE

This is the night, what it does to you. I had nothing to offer anybody except my own confusion. —Jack Kerouac

Because I make things up
I told her I thought we could call the coyotes
and since I had listened so closely
I *yip yip yipped* first like they do
and then tipped my head back to sail
a held note out into the valley.

It was the night of her mother's funeral
and we were in the yard on borrowed quilts
and it was July and the stars were swollen
and low. My howl made her laugh

which made me laugh, and I told her
we needed to sound like a pack, and then
she howled with me.

This is the night, what it did to us,
and it was the first time
they answered.

INVOLUNTARY ACTION

Choose to govern
blink and breath

and later, forgetting, they will resume
their natural action unattended.

The heart, however, chugs
on the same old track.

My neighbor wants
to walk with me, she says

cardiac trouble compels her
to go slow

and stop often. Behind
the house, fox kits jump

straight up in the sun,
dash under a diagonal

of logs. The chest rises
and falls with a caged tide,

sometimes labored and caught,
ragged or shallow.

Palpitations are nothing more
than the pulse felt.

I assure her
I trust her heart.

MAY THAT LIGHT BE MY AUTHORITY

After Deborah Shore

I have pledged and knelt
and I have raised my hands
above my head

washed myself in blood
and allowed the wafer to dissolve
upon my tongue.

I have slept all night on an island
underneath the heron rookery,

tied prayers
made of colored paper
to the limbs of trees

and filled tablets
with gratitude's documentation.

I have been to the powwow
and worn a medicine bag
stout with quartz.

I have celebrated
in the services of scotch
and tobacco

and one night in Wyoming
I drove with no headlamps.

I have dragged
a dead badger from the water
and I have told lies.
Following my own breath

leads me down a staircase
in an apartment building
where I once lived.
I watched the wrecker
cave in the sides
on the day they took it down,

but still in meditation
I count backwards from ten
as I go down those stairs—

five counts to the landing
and turn. One time the door
at the bottom opened

onto a dark field, plowed.
In the distance a bonfire.

Sabbatical

Turning away from people,
I enter instead the den of the muskrat
burrowed into the bank,

the teardrop nest of oriole
suspended from a thin branch
overhanging the fen.

Sleeping out,
I distinguish one coyote voice
from another

and hear the bullfrogs
swing the rusty gate of their call.
The two-toed deer

have stopped fleeing me
now that all I carry is a broken piece

of pottery. A brace of drakes
and hens dive the pond.

I traded telephone calls
for a litter of fox kits bounding
the hill.

A neighbor raises guinea fowl,
but having turned away from people

I have no duty to warn. I study
signature eyeshine.

The sun naps on last year's
grass blades, and the plexus
of dirt roads has gone soft with rain.

Rarely Have We Seen a Person Fail

I have not come to sobriety without reason.
The rim of the glass itself insisted. I was collared by bottles
let loose from their cardboard cells, who brandished photographs
of my unborn children. The clerk, crushing a cigarette
behind the liquor store counter, clucked his tongue
at my purchases. How could I continue,
when the cubed ice hurled curses
from the cradle of my palm?

I have not come to sobriety
of my own accord. And no one does. The alchemy failed.
Weary of medicating the problem
with larger and larger doses of the problem, even I
could see the futility. I tried to persist,
learned to vomit in order to make more room
in my stomach, to prime before events,
to hold one hand with the other, to interlock
day and night. But longing has distended
itself beyond my reach. My organs have drafted
armies and built fences at their borders, a yellow dog
has rubbed against my skin.

I have not come to sobriety without quarrel. Tarot
cards foretold a better outcome. I knew the mixers
were the culprit. Stringing Jacob's Ladder
full of promises hasn't quelled the gag reflex, and now
my hands are tied. Otherwise I'd raise them
over my head. Otherwise I would have already surrendered.

EXTRACTING

The man pissing against the side of the house
says the world is too tender, says
he'd have been here sooner
but the bridge is out and the rail cars
slammed shut years ago.

His life rotted early,
but despite that he bought a time share
in Branson. Which was fine
until the power died and a freezer
of venison went bad, stunk
like the morgue ever after.

He's seen a few things, let's say.
The inside of thirty or forty
southern county jails. And if he has
enough drinks, he'll tell anyone
where the breed went green.

Can't wear watches, they stop
on him. Used to live in a rut shack
next to the Big Muddy, and would
still but for the snakes.
Grew cantaloupe and gave it away,
doesn't even like it but likes
to raise it. Once he wrecked a car—
the engine block pushed through
the dash, the jaws of life
fifty minutes extracting him,
but he brushed off and walked away,
a little headached behind the eyes
all he noticed. It was a '67 Mustang.
So much chrome on that thing.
Man, that was one hell of a car.

Being Young

Means being gold leaf, the raised
eyebrow, a laborer
who isn't book smart, someone
who can put an injured dog down.

Means a faceted vase
filled with pursed blooms.

It means being able to smoke,
a rampage of circling
elephants guarding
the carcass of the villager
they have trampled.

Trampling, itself.
And digging a trench for protection.
These, too, are of the young.

Along with suturing, spelling,
the ridge formed across a wound.
Standing at the end of a dirt road,
not making eye contact,
a word scratched into paint.
Outboard motors. The canal of the ear.
The way we say *intact*.

It means the red haired man
yelling from the cab of the truck,
but not the torn map. Not the broken
tooth, the stained reunion, not
the close room.

Instead, being young
is the gun shot, the leap,
the upspear. It is off kilter
and uncut. It is the bed

unmade and slept in again,
the portage, the missing
guard rail, all the trash talk.
It is coil, locker room,
repetitions, helium balloon
released. Not keeping your head
down, no mention of
customer service, no parakeets
enclosed in dainty bars.

It means rapids,
contest, bee hive, high walls, sling
shot, travesty, ruthless.
Not palpitate, not convert
or eloquence, not filter.

Being young
is tang. Shine. Heap.
Not sled, not holster.

It means voice.
Not rheum.

BOY WALKING AHEAD OF TRAIN

Between the rails, face turned away,
he fails to respond to the horn.

Trains take miles to brake.

The engineer considers a jump to the ground
to sprint ahead and throw him off the tracks,
but no person could outrun this story.

It was music that the walker heard,
instead of warning —
two cups at his ears, a fine cord, a silver disk.

Behind him, something fast and black.

ODE TO LIGHT

This is to light reflecting from the polished nail
of a high school girl who has skipped class
to sit at the edge of a marsh and let frogs
sing her to sleep.

To light reflecting off the green shingles
of her house, where she has stored her baby teeth
in a music box. To light reflecting off the hood
of her boyfriend's car, a dark green Buick
he got cheap from his uncle. This is to light

shining back at her from the pin setter
at the bowling alley, her shoes laced too tight
as she lifts the ball and takes two steps forward.

This is to the tinsel light of her hair, the bead
reflected from her earring. This is to light

from the dashboard of his car shining on the map
so they can point at any little place
and go there.

THE AGED PRIEST GIVES THE HOMILY

A great blue heron stands on a stone pedestal
in the center of a small body of water.

On the bank a row of chairs,
each a replica of an electric chair,

and together we will go and sit
with our tablets on our laps, eyes forward.

And the bird will face us and begin
to teach. The lesson today is about tricking

the mind, about a flick of light, about
the studied movement of schools of fish.

You may wander off in thought to dividing
your parents' things, to the hospital corridor,

the greed of others. But here in the shallow
water is where we learn focus enough to be

unerring, to be still. When it is time to throw
the spear, the whole of the body participates

like that of the man, strapped down and hooded,
when the terrible connection is made.

THEY ASK WHY I STAY

I tell them it is the quality of life.
Low crime, affordable housing, good
schools is what they think I mean—
the rope that phrase-makers loop
so harmlessly around our throats
that we think it is a ribbon, dangling
a medal of citizenship or justice
or free speech on our chests.

Instead it is the grasshopper,
sunfish yellow, that my husband
said was big as a mouse, and it was,
awkwardly walking the rung
of the wisteria's ladder against
the peeling paint of the garage.
How the neighbor thought to point
it out to us, and how we both looked
when he did, and agreed it was
the biggest we had ever seen.
It is the slam of wooden screen door
into its frame. Window glass so heavy
it long since broke its cording,
dropped the counterbalance weights
inside the plaster walls, and how we
have to prop them open now
with a can of green beans or a hanger.
It is the *grate grate grate* of cicada
in late summer, so loud we have to
raise our voices on the porch swing.
It is the way the climbing rose
has thrown her arms across
both living room windows, pressing
thorns and blooms against the glass
for our approval. It is that
when she does, we give it.

Why I Waited For You

After Susan Elbe

Because in a hollow space in my twenties
a day turned over on itself like a sowbug
and I saw the curve of your full name.

Because when your mother
used her perfect penmanship
to document the first foods you tasted,
the shadow of a woman
whose head and neck were shaped like mine
pressed against the page.

Because when I rowed the wooden boat
on the lake at night until my arms tired,
a magnificent bird just above me
let loose one long wing feather into the hull
and I knew you were coming.

Because when our fingertips rested
on the marker of the Ouija board,
it spilled out a history
we knew we could claim.

When it asked our intentions,
my pores filled with scent from an orchard
long ago axed and burned. Still, the cherry blossoms
made a bed for us, familiar as my own tongue
resting on the back of my teeth.

Every long day behind me
left in a row, like a trail I could follow backwards,
I hunted the dark roads for you before I knew
I knew you, because the porch swing wanted your weight,
the dog whined for your low-voiced direction,
the cherries waited for the warmth
of your open, then closing, mouth.

PHOSPHORESCENCE

My father's work in the war was classified,
but now I know
what it takes to shape clouds to drown
the routes of tanks, the chemical mix
that builds thunderheads.

I am the flickering light
over marshland, the cupped nest
in a felled tree.

My father's medicine
keeps me young. At night
I dream of fields of transition.
See the high windows in the train station.
Put your name on the waiting list
in the hospital lobby.

A boy I knew, the one who smashed
a windshield with his fists,
tells me he has been married
sixteen years now, works all day
in the laundromat. The boy I knew
remembered my dad as fierce. He removes
pictures from his soft wallet—
a daughter in a tutu, a boy with a wide grin.

My dad put his hands together and made clouds.
He could not say. Back then he could not say
he was only the weatherman.

He Leaves, She Stays

There are snakes coiled in the toilet
tank, but I still remember security,
the smell in the house after food
had been slow cooked.

After I defended myself and was sure
I could not continue, you nailed thin
boards to hold the rotted ceiling in place.
Something greater came and loomed
above me, the musical light
of stars, and I was awake
for many days. When the sirens sounded
we did not take shelter, love,
we went out to the dark yard
to stare at the spin cloud.

It's over. I am smashing the last glass
in the white sink. If you were here I'd yell
something fortuitous. If you
need me, I'll be in a cave
made by throwing our bedclothes
over the tabletop, I'll be in there
reading Rumi to the dog
until the end days. You are still
welcome here, though you are
always silvered and whispering. My knees
have given in, and the dog cowers,
but these are your walls, your grace.
These are your dirty little walls.

CATAMOUNT

She came to the party
as a lion, and promptly killed
the three young women dressed
as Playboy bunnies. Because her tongue
was specialized for scraping meat
from bone, she stripped their bodies
to ribbons. She came to

the party as a lion and barefoot,
her retractable claws absent
from her prints. She came to the party
although it was against her nature,
and asked them to turn down
the lights. Men commented
to one another on the contracted
vertical slits in her eyes.
She wore a cinnamon coat
that she did not remove. She came
to the party as a lion and no one was amused
when she marked the edges of the room.
One flash of her carnassial teeth
stemmed the outcry.

When the conversation bore
cornered her, she leapt straight up
and balanced on the china hutch.
By the end of the night,
oblivious to the drama, she denned
in the space beneath the desk, and guests
held their coats above their heads
as they backed slowly out to the street.

Twenty-Five Years Later, She Learns Her Ex is Dying

Five nights in succession she recalled him in dreams.
His voice was a series of clicks and whistles,
the sound of Burlington Northern Santa Fe
troubling the long rails. If she starts to walk
those tracks, her cupboard doors will spill
their store of crackers and oats onto the floor,
her shingles slip from the sure grasp of the roof.
Linoleum plans to stall her. The dog knows
to sigh and paw the water bowl. Her climbing
rose has been positioning itself all summer.

Still, she remembers herself as a sundress
waving from a make-shift clothesline on the fire escape
of a red brick building. Or as a banner of blonde hair
advertising from the back of a black motorcycle.
She wants to take up cigarettes again, sleepwalk,
lose both shoes at a party in a neighboring town.
She wants to tell him something, or sing a chorus
of that old Donovan song to him, maybe just over
the phone. She remembers shuffling the Tarot cards,
intuiting a future much more wondrous than the thud
of news on her narrow porch, the civil greetings
penned to college friends. She wants something old,
something stolen. She wants to balance on that rail
as though she were not an owner of things, as though
the train was due, as though everything still mattered.

BLACK DUCK

There is a day like a cathedral
made of wax, a day when the low flying planes
make you think of warfare, of Blitzkrieg,
of ruins. Or sometimes they make you
think of cartoons you watched in childhood,
the smart aleck rabbit too cool for death—
the long stick of a rifle threaded down the hole,
but trickster is standing by the tree behind the hunter.

May we all be. May we all get to look
over the shoulder as someone takes aim.
May we all learn the fox trot, cross our legs in repose,
ride the tricycle with the oversized front wheel.

There is a woman sweeping her wooden porch.
She is listening to the radio.
She mouths the words to these old songs.
She doesn't hear the planes.

A man pretending to be a cowboy
sings about the range.
He is staying in the best hotel in town.
He is taking surfing lessons.

See a woman
with a packet of letters
and a match. There is a rolled up
carpet by the street. She has emptied
her rooms of everything
except one chair with a broken leg.

There is a black sputtering duck
in a pan on the stove. Steam is rising
but he is still negotiating,
he is placating,
he is getting warmer.

My stomach cannot stomach this.
He is not real and I am
worried about his temperature.
Tactically speaking, I am worried about
how he will get out of the pan, the freezer,
the trap. I am worried because
I have never seen him fly.

POWER OUTAGE ON A CLOUDED MOONLESS NIGHT

Every lit thing now dark
at the center and the edges, no coil of hibernating
brightness that saved itself through torpor or feigned death.

The rectangle of valanced glass
now no different than the lathe and plaster
around it, the near and far away

equally obscured. The proverbial hand waving
before the face might as well be bats in remote caverns.
Dark moves against the shoulder of dark

as we have faith in, and attend to, the accretion
of other faculties, as we palm and tap,
eavesdrop, sample and sip the edge of known things.

BIRTHDAY

The black calf is two hours on the barn floor
resisting the nudge to rise and walk.

In the house above the barn yard
every light is shining. A boy who flew

kites all afternoon is blowing out
candles and hamming for the camera.

Plates piled in the sink, thick with frosting,
are set aside to thaw colostrum

under the running hot water. The calf
was a good weight, and is out of the weather.

The family is singing to the boy. The calf
has no spirit for this world.

TARANTULA FIRE
-for Jeff

A boy far away experiments with paralysis,
using tiny doses of tarantula venom.

The sky won't hold a kite today
so the man from over the hill

asks permission. He wants
to set his fields on fire.

Thousands of disguised beetles
line my windows.

They are never what I think they are.
He wants to stem the cedar,

and burn before the nests are made.
This is a small farmhouse

and the barn in the yard is decades dry.
The spider immobilizes her prey

and this is what draws the boy to her.
I don't know what I'm agreeing to.

There are seeds waiting in the soil here
that can't crack open without fire.

He tells me the large trees go unscathed.
Without my yes he cannot move.

He implies the neighbors to the south and east
are ready to burn. I am tired

of making decisions. The tarantula breathes
through book lungs made of thin sheets

of tissue folded into pages. My own breathing
has been ragged of late.

The deer and leverets will flee and return
when the ground cools.

I stand on my doorstep ready to say
light this valley, or don't.

The tarantula's blood is not true
blood, and her heart is a slender tube.

I light matches and shake them out
to smell the sulfur; only burning

keeps the understory at bay.
Frozen, I have to vote

for equilibrium. I'll stand in the road
when fire overtakes the hillside

and mark the woods emptying themselves.
The boy is moving into the future

on the venom. He will
make medicine out of fear.

MUSTER

My father stationed states away,
my father at Air War College.
My father on reel to reel tape.

My father's pressed blue uniforms.
Green zippered flight suit.

My father the navigator.
My father's dissertation
specifying the movement of tornadoes
across the Great Plains. My father
with shotguns, with lures, with leave.

My father TDY, on alert, my father
seeding clouds with dry ice. My father
deciphering ocean currents. My father

during the Cuban missile crisis, my father
at my crib. My father with elephants,
my father of six continents. My father
at Global Weather.

My child father escaping the landlord's
eviction, my father thin and pious. My father's
rote memory, his passive vocabulary. My father
and stocks, and driving lessons. My father
of the scotch and water.

My father's replacement valves. My father stockpiling.
My father of favors, of payment. My father's
shoe shine kit, my father with a needle nosed pliers.
My father the colonel.

My father deliberating. My father's father
afraid of wind. My father's balcony.
My father's match head,

my father's ticks. My father with rheumatic
fever, my father's scarred heart.

My father
of languages, my father of Strategic
Air Command, of body surfing. My father
of peel-your-own shrimp, of templates.

My father's wild poems. My
father's quarters, his black wallet. My
father's blackmail, my father at the blackjack
table. My father superior, my father
weeping. My father's property. My father's limbs
and torso, my father on the gurney, my father's salute.

Memory as Lighthouse, Memory as Bomb

They told me I would not remember
but the rootholds of the mind are rigorous.

Amnesia is not a choice, not a warranty of anesthetic,
not the brain's sophisticated segregation

of experience deemed injurious to function.
Rather it is the story of the vessel arriving in the bay

that we cannot see because we do not know *ship*
but do know disturbance on the surface

and if we peer and puzzle at the water's strange course
the craft comes into view, a miraculous assembling.

Once comprehension rives them, we cannot see
the woman's face and the image of the vase as one.

The memory center may be flooded with the medicated
smoke that expects to still the hive, to lure

the soldiers into dereliction of duty but even so
the trip-trap footsteps of the hunched figure

ascending the 210 stairs of the lighthouse
continue their rhythm. I cannot forget

the truth revealing itself, a disturbance of flow
and then stunning materialization,

a brilliance like bombs exploding,
a white light that sears the skull and throbs

in the chemical reuptake between cells,
replicating history, insisting on full recollection.

All Night, That Turning

Stars above a ship
that slowly pivots.
All night, that turning against
the ocean's resistance.

A sea otter has lost
her pup. It drifted
when she went below
to gather abalone
and urchins. Sinking
is impossible, the newborn
lanugo buoyant as kapok.

A man's hands
cup a cigarette
on the deck. He stands
at the railing. He never
wanted children.

The din of engine deceives.
No progress can be made
until the turn is complete.

The otter searches
but the baby is out
of range. The man
is hotboxing and dizzy.

There is no such thing as rescue.

Born in the House of Love

Tree limbs groaned aside
to make way. The salt river poured
over my head. My iris constricted
without knowing that it could.

Still I wasted my body
on the world. Handed my keys to men
with mud clamped to their boots.
Drew putty into my air sacs,
holding my breath until it dried.
Turned the soft crook of my arm up
to the needle's bite. Rode on the shoulders
of drunken boys who could not
keep their balance in the dark.

We are each holier than we know,
tumbling ourselves against tectonic edges
like glass beads, clearing and clarifying
until the world, when the light has a certain slant,
can see its unguarded face right through us.

My Brother's Wedding

There's the usual sheep march down the center
aisle, a bad soloist, canned vows.
Afterward we are Nikoned and Cannoned
and shuffled left, repositioned
like stems. *Okay now the groom*
and the ring bearer—where is the ring
bearer? Later, the bride's father
drunk at the microphone, breathing
too heavily into the amplification.
And he is giving a toast, or should
be, but instead he is reading a joke
that he printed from his email, a joke
or a touching story, one that ends
in angels. I am up to my ass
in good behavior, pacified and placid
while the rutting common asshole
is taking up all my oxygen. The best man
will need to wipe the mike down
afterwards, make some creative segue
into stories about my brother
that shouldn't be told here. My own stories
are my own, and I have followed him
so long I know the outline of his back
like the design of my nail bed, the half
moons rising. We are Indian scouts on saw
horses, Arctic rescuers arriving by sled,
tribal divers from the high cliff
of municipality. Never has there been
a place I wouldn't follow him. The warrior
in him requires a better tradition
than what has been piecemealed together,
a ceremonial fire rather than a dollar
dance, one cello playing from the deep
hillside instead of the Macarena. He
is turning himself around under the disco ball,
and although the room is dark, I catch his eye
and raise my hand, waving.

A LIE I WILL TELL YOU

It is recessed so completely—a nail head pounded below the board—
that when asked to recall my first house, its orange brick or blackening roof,
I see the house next door instead, or smell cinnamon dissolving
in morning light, a bridge that memory shuttles over and back like a late season
honey bee, dizzy with pollen from aster and rose of Sharon.

The past is a cardboard carton filled with movie reels in gray canisters
that I work to pry open and play, the projector stuttering dust as the shot
of light shows the stolen features, full and dimensional against white slate.
But the film has deteriorated and everything soft is gone, leaving only
the street name, pop tops, fire ring. If I never remember, I was never there.

I was born in the house of love. I slept in a willow cradle. No baby ever
was smaller or more whole. I had words in my mouth, full and smooth
as rocks lifted from the river bed, and all around me the men and women
raised sticks, no, voices, raised voices in a chant I can almost hear in that
hammock of sleep just before waking. I wore a sweater embroidered with poems.

We know this isn't true. But truth is a rusting prop plane in the upper meadow
that has been grounded since the bank failed, or the crop, or the marriage.
And I cannot raise it from its ligature of trumpet vine. I do not see the place
I came from, despite the hammer's claw wedged under the edge of the nail
head, grinding the wood beneath it until the grain is feathered.
I was born in the house of love.

AFTER THE TEST SAID YES

Stopped at the crossroad on 14th street, ice clean
as an apple slice under my wheels, I am waiting
for my turn and I don't know yet about looking back
which is why I cannot describe the color or make of what hit me,
moving too fast to brake on the black, and my blue Volkswagen
shoots out into oncoming lanes and once there begins to spin—
and that is where time slows, like they always say,
forming an opening in the day that was already thick with news.

The man comes to the car window,
wants to know if I'm okay, and I tell him I'm pregnant,
that I just found out this morning, and he looks like he will faint,
and I open the door and step out into the street.

And this, I believe, is the story of conception: how my daughter
used momentum and ice and velocity and impact
to pierce the atmosphere and enter the world.

Ishi Comes Down from the Canyon

In 1911, after the last of his family had died, and decades after his tribe was thought to be extinct, an aboriginal "wild man" walked out of the remote canyon where he had been living in northern California. He came to be called Ishi, which meant man, after refusing to say his own name.

Dark moves against the shoulder of dark
as we attend to the accretion
of other faculties, as we palm and tap,
sample and sip the edge of known things.

Dark at the center and dark at the edges,
no coil of hibernating brightness that saved itself
through torpor or feigned death.
The inner linings dark, each larynx
snapped shut. Even the depressor on the tongue,
the strangled ah, done in darkness.

Dark speaks unto dark
in a language unintelligible, a grinding
of surfaces, and we are all ears, all
eavesdrop and hush. But this is a dark
there is no translation for, the underside,
the crook, the fig not yet tunneled by wasp.

Dark where we tramp out a circle
before lying down, where anything blessed
is clasped. Darkness such as the hair
of a woman unplaited and dropped,
curtaining the world. It is remote
controlled dark, factory made,
assembled elsewhere.

Darkness spreads out like oil
and weights every wing, and we push back
with our thin voices, our child swords
raised. Hooping around us, spilling over
the dam, darkness toils at the lip
of the canyon, contaminates the marsh,
abolishes history. With every known
thing annulled, Ishi decides.

ISHI SPEAKS

Later they will say I was starved
and though it is true I had grown thin
this did not compel me. I knew scarcity
as a brother and a guide.

Did you think I didn't anticipate
the mockery? How could I be anything
but foolish? I knew they would smell
my breath, that they would press
the ends of my fingers into ink.

Of course many had died
in the canyon and I had said words
above them. Though I moved
into a high crevice, I came down
to visit the bones. Sometimes I spoke
in the old way to the beautiful
hoop of ribs, but eventually
they each fell inward. One whole
day I laid in the stream. The clouds
moved their dark shapes across
my skin and I learned to forget.

You may think it is my duty
to remember, but I do not value
recollection. It is work
that is never done, and serves no one.

You want my stories, my ways.
These things are cached in rock.
I came down not for food,
your slimy gruel with its foreign flavor.

I came because your odd speech,
which I still cannot comprehend,
called me down, the voices especially

of your children, the way
they yawn and sing. I came to listen
to the sounds that rise from your throats
that had left the canyon deafening.

NEBRASKA

Here, we understand that shadows fold their wings and settle down
in midday, tucked underfoot like a coyote den the unschooled never
notice. We can see a fire in the next county, the smoke a thundercloud
of blackbirds twirling for fall, grouping and regrouping themselves
as though to remember something already lost, washed out
and splayed in the wet clay of the creek bed. You can drive
an entire afternoon here and not see a person, but all the way
the meadowlarks will be opening the doors of their throats,
letting out music like milkweed seeds delivered downwind.
You might start counting those birds after awhile, picture them
as mile markers on the telephone wires, wondering if you've seen
the same one over and over again. We have more stars here, so many
that strangers think there is something wrong with our sky, that it's
fake or that Sioux women have beaded our night with constellations
not seen in Minneapolis or Memphis, fresh ones that we can give
names to as we lie on the hood of the car. We can call one *Mountain
Lion Reclaims Ancestral Home*, after the cougar who roamed up
a wooded thicket into Omaha this fall, ranging until the zoo director
shot him with a tranquilizer dart. Here we can keep naming star puzzles
until the threat of sunrise blues the black space above us.
This is a place for things that take time, the long stitching together
of soft spots in the heart, the wind across the Missouri River Valley
scooping loess into hills unlike any others on this continent,
seeds stored in the cellar of the prairie for a hundred years
patient for fire, unable to crack themselves open without it.
This is a place where disappointments deep as aquifer
can spill themselves out, fill up and empty again, as many times
as the wound requires. This is a place where a person can heal,
or choose not to heal. We have both kinds.

After Buying the Property

You take the door off
and broom the stairwell

before bowing into
the root cellar.

You yell up
about it being wet

and describe old
coffee cans

filled with hypodermics.
I find the light switch.

Shelves of rotted wood
line the brick wall.

Glass has gone dark
with peaches and beets

and green with pickles.
She's been dead

since 1988. Her addict
son dead ten years.

In a brown jar
with a narrow opening

a mouse skeleton,
his teeth tiny rows

of beadwork.
Here is her wash pan.

Here is his
stash.

PORCUPINE

You think we are the pointed argument,
the man drunk at the party showing off
his gun collection, the bed of nettles.

What we really are is hidden from you:
girl weeping in the closet among her stepfather's boots;
tuft of rabbit fur caught in barbed wire; body of the baby
in the landfill; boy with the shy mouth playing his guitar
at the picnic table, out in the dirt yard.

We slide into this world benign and pliable,
quills pressed down smooth over back and tail.
Only one hour here stiffens the barbs into thousands
of quick retorts. Everything this well-guarded
remembers being soft once.

OCCUPATION

Pay attention. It is all about paying attention.
— Susan Sontag

For two weeks I have been watching the badger
decay at the fence line, a walk over
the dam and down the deer path.

In the first week vultures
circled but wouldn't raid, as though
poison tainted the kill. They have
stopped approaching.

Horizontal snow on Friday
slowed her collapse, but today she blooms
with a pocket of white worms, furiously
climbing over one another.

Soon I will return to my old life,
the windows closed, the blue light
flickering in the living room.

I cannot explain adoration, the strange
homage paid by watching flesh and fur
fall from the architecture of bones.

This is my work, the watching.
The maggots cannot say, nor the vultures,
how they came to their work, and
I cannot say how mine was assigned to me.
Even the body ripped apart
at the edge of the field
is doing its work, sweetening
the air, marking time, reminding.

GLOAM

There is a wheel
in the world

green with lichen
and wet with blood
and semen.

Fish spawn in the shallows
and the badger
rots on the bank.

My children
are typing their messages
and driving late into the night

while time pounds her feet
over and over
on the compact clay.

Loss
does its damp
unfurling.

CONFESSION OF FAITH

When I remembered how to pray
the elm branches had already developed their dark streaks.
The bruise of northern lights flared,
and the wind heaved the sides of my canvas tent.
How long had I been traveling? My sisters
had launched into the river years ago, and eggs cooled
in the nests. My arm ached from throwing rocks into the water,

and when queried, the prophet laughed with a choking sound
and picked glass from his feet. I remained on the bank
because of some way the water swirled, the intoxicating
effect of current. All day I would lie on an old mattress
and play melodies on my mouth organ. I needed to know

how so much water could be on the move and mute.
The bread I carried went blue with age, and my hair grew down
to the blades protruding from my back. All night
the elm bark beetles packed up illness,
bearing it like gifts to the next tree.

I'd like to say it happened in a factory,
at an ornate altar, in a rail car. I'd like to tell you
I came out of isolation to look at the faces of people,
to have them clasp my shoulders and tell me the news.

The truth is prayer came to me in a beetle,
with my ear pressed to the trunk, where the Lakota man
said there is a tinkling voice, a music being made
inside of old trees. Prayer stopped being a puzzle
and became a boat made of bark with a lantern swung over
the side. That is how I left the wide river. I am not writing this
down for you, I know already it cannot be replicated.
But when they say I did not believe,
point to the dazzle of light on the overside of leaves.
Open your hand and show them the beetle.

BEYOND THIS LIFE

Ask her to set fruit out to scent the table
as nightfall turns the trees white.
We will be coming in. We have bent
to our work for a moon's cycle, lifting
heaven from the field. Look back
over the cleared vineyard, where the sun
wells yellow against the horizon.

We go about in our angel disguises,
acting as though there is a trap door
in the graveyard. Finally, enough work

has been chiseled away that we can breathe,
though something cries from the edge
of the woods, and we find we are far from the house.
Before we go in, where the room is red with love,
explain something to me. Teach me
your foreign alphabet, and I will split
a walnut to reveal the ace of hearts.

Reliquary

Always I am taking the wounded from the mouth of the hungry,
the wet fur of the leveret from the jaws of the hound.

Or I am the one with the sledgehammer, the poisoned steak
that I slip over the fence after every authority refused
to quarantine the beast. I have to protect my own,

  but the world assigns too many to me,
says they are each my own, the lobsters in the tank
at the market, the sparrows in the neighbor's trap,
the massive tawniness at the edge of the field at dusk.

  I love the world that wants to eat me,
and I crave to devour it, too—smear my face with butter and grease,
talk into the night about meals I've had.

  I am the paralyzed rescuer,
watching the nest mown over, waving from the porch
as the men head off with their long guns. If I have been sent here
for some task, I have blundered, I have failed.
I couldn't find the trap door, the men with the proper authority.

Yet I rest my feet in the stream and it washes me anyway,
and birds make nests of ribbons in my eaves. I am sorry. I was ill
equipped. I can't even tell you I will do better.

  But I will collect the bones, I will stand
at the roadside and say your names: *Porcupine, Mule Deer, Wildcat.*
I will take what lasts longest, the jaw bone set with jewels,
let it bleach in the white heat.

  I will say I knew you, that I found it by Salt Creek,
or in the Big Horns. I will show the architecture of your mouth
to children. I will let them run their fingertips, whorled with identity,
over the tops of your marvelous teeth.

EARTH BEHIND ME, BLUE AND BRIGHT

Reject the tunnel told by others,
the finish of radiant beams, the beloved
escort, the arms of mother.
Let imagination be the vehicle for dying.
Let's say it is a dog shaking water from her coat,
who wets the clothes of those who stand here, crying.
Or maybe it could be the campfire's sound
when the men who built it rise to move along
and douse it from above. Or a song sung in rounds
that always begins again as soon as it is ending.
A crate of pheasants hatched and old enough
to be released into the fields. We think of it as sending,
the way we get from one place to another,
the transport of the special DNA or Higher Self
we picture as eternal. It could be a hand that smothers
or a tamping down until we can't be found.
We want a grander place, the brush with God!
But at the grave we cannot help but eye the mound
of dirt, though it is covered by a tarp, and worry
over its weight and density. Let's say the end
is clay mixing with water, a slurry
of our insoluble parts. Or the church bells
just before the clapper strikes. A lowering
of rope into a cavern, the smell
of minerals, the wheeze of your own breath.
It's opening a book, or falling forward,
it's death biting the tail of its own death.

This collection was assisted by the support of many, including Amy Plettner, Marjorie Saiser, T. Marni Vos, Karen Gettert Shoemaker, Jaimes Alsop, Virginia Thompson, Deb Walz, Mike Harrell, Mark Sanders, Rex Walton, Greg Kosmicki, Greg Kuzma, Justin Evans, Grace Bauer, Jeremy Halinen, Twyla Hansen, Lynne Lang, Susan Elbe, Diane Wells, Marianne Zarzana, Heidi Hermanson, Lori Folts, Mary Madigan, Paul Gerber, Sherry O'Keefe, Roxanna McLaughlin, Barbara Schmitz, Michael Hoard, Eric Erlandson, Jaime Hackbart, Duke Engel, Aleta Braun, Ann Chwatsky, Cindy Fleener, Evan Peterson, Karla Decker, Mari Nansel, Patricia McInroy, Marianne Woeppel, Dale Novak, Kimberly Verhines, Laura Davis, Lauren Hawkins, Paige Namuth, Deborah Shore, and the poets of the Gazebo.

I am grateful for the steady and heartfelt support extended to me from Tara and Ben Polly, Margot Erlandson, and my loved ones in Minnesota, Colorado, Florida and Monona County.

The core poems in this collection were written during the time-outside-of-time experience provided by Jentel, an artist residency program in rural Wyoming. One of the fellow residents, Aleta Braun, was working in a studio in sight of my cabin window, and every day she'd set paintings and collages out in the sun, against the building. Her work became an evolving part of the landscape for the month we were there together. One of those paintings serves as a cover image for this collection.

Time, freedom and funding was provided by the Kimmel Harding Nelson Center for the Arts, Jentel Artist Residency, Brush Creek Foundation for the Arts, the Nebraska Arts Council, and the National Endowment for the Arts.

ACKNOWLEDGMENTS

Grateful acknowledgment to the editors of the following publications, where these poems or versions of them first appeared: "Offering," *The Ecopoetry Anthology*, Trinity University Press, 2013; "Muster," "Confession of Faith," "He Leaves, She Stays," and "Power Outage on a Clouded, Moonless Night," *The Untidy Season*, Backwaters Press, 2013; "Ishi Speaks," *A Face to Meet the Faces: An Anthology of Contemporary Persona Poetry*, University of Akron Press, 2012; "Occupation," *Knockout*, Spring 2012; "Coyote," *Terrain. org*, Spring/Summer 2011; "Sabbatical," *South Dakota Review*, Summer 2010; "Being Young," *Apalachee Review*, Issue 61; "Tarantula Fire," *Prism Review*, 2010; "After Buying the Property," *Two Review*, 2010; "Offering," and "Boy Walking Ahead of Train," *Knockout*, Spring 2010; "Catamount," and "May That Light Be My Authority," *Hawk & Whippoorwill*, Winter 2010; "Extracting," *Southern California Review*, Fall 2009; "The Aged Priest Gives the Homily," "Beyond this Life," *Cerise Press*, Fall/Winter 2009; "Memory as Lighthouse, Memory as Bomb," *Qarrtsiluni*, Fall 2008; "Phosphorescence," *Southern California Review*, Fall 2008; "Gloam," "Another Word for Leaving," and "Black Duck," *Hobble Creek Review*, 2008; "Mnemosyne's Mausoleum," and "Porcupine," *Prairie Schooner*, Summer 2007; "The Onset of Memory," *Smartish Pace*, Issue 14, April 2007; "Quitting," and "Reliquary," *Eleventh Muse*, 2007; "Rarely Have We Seen a Person Fail," *32 Poems*, Volume 5, Issue 1, 2007; "Twenty-five Years Later, She Learns Her Ex is Dying," *Natural Bridge*, Spring 2006; "All Night, That Turning," and "Earth Behind Me, Blue and Bright," *Apalachee Review*, Number 56, 2006; "Instead of Telling," *The Florida Review*, Spring 2005; "Why I Waited for You," and "A Lie I Will Tell You," *MARGIN*, Winter 2005; "Born in the House of Love," *Puerto del Sol*, Spring 2005; "Nebraska," *The Massachusetts Review*, Winter 2004-2005; "Before She Decides," *Anthology One*, Alsop Review, 2004; "They Ask Why I Stay," *South Dakota*

Review, Winter 2003/2004; "After the Test Said Yes," *Barrow Street*, Winter 2003.

Poems from this collection have been reprinted in *Best New Poets 2007, Nebraska Presence, Garrison Keillor's Writers' Almanac, Skirt!,* and *Miller's Pond.* The poem "Occupation" won the International Reginald Shepherd Memorial Poetry Prize, and "Tarantula Fire" won the Prism Review Poetry Prize.

CPSIA information can be obtained at www.ICGtesting.com
Printed in the USA
LVOW13s0524250813

349458LV00004B/216/P